What Is a Hundred?

by Danielle Carroll

Consultant: Brad Laager, MA, Math Educator
Little Falls Community Middle School

Yellow
Umbrella
Books
for early readers

Yellow Umbrella Books are published by Red Brick Learning
7825 Telegraph Road, Bloomington, Minnesota 55438
http://www.redbricklearning.com

Editorial Director: Mary Lindeen
Senior Editor: Hollie J. Endres
Senior Designer: Gene Bentdahl
Photo Researcher: Signature Design
Developer: Raindrop Publishing
Consultant: Brad Laager, MA, Math Educator, Little Falls Community School
Conversion Assistants: Jenny Marks, Laura Manthe

Library of Congress Cataloging-in-Publication Data
Carroll, Danielle
  What Is a Hundred? / by Danielle Carroll
     p. cm.
  Includes index.
  ISBN 0-7368-5860-1 (hardcover)
  ISBN 0-7368-5290-5 (softcover)
  1. Counting—Juvenile literature. 2. Hundred (The number)—Juvenile literature. I. Title.
  QA113.C3778 2005
  513.2'11—dc22

                                                         2005016140

Photo Credits:
Cover: SuperStock; Title Page and Pages 2–7: Signature Design; Page 8: Kevin Fleming/Corbis;
Page 9: Rick Doyle/Corbis; Pages 10 and 11: Signature Design; Page 12: Alan Schein/Corbis;
Page 13: Richard B. Levine/Photographer Showcase; Page 14: Kim Eriksen/Corbis

1 2 3 4 5 6 11 10 09 08 07 06

Table of Contents

Count to 100

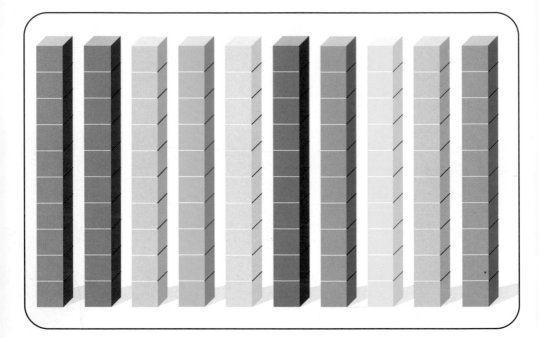

The number 100 is a big number. It has three **digits**. The **number words** for 100 are *one hundred*.

You can count to 100 by ones. It takes a long time to reach 100 this way, but you can do it!

Counting 1 by 1 is a way to count numbers. One penny means 1 cent. When you have 100 pennies, they **equal** a 1 dollar bill.

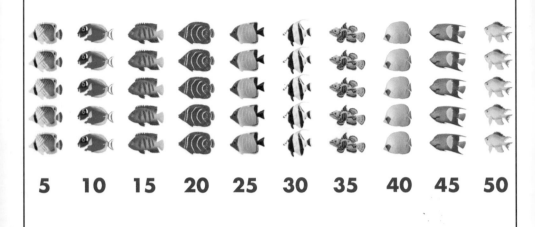

| 5 | 10 | 15 | 20 | 25 | 30 | 35 | 40 | 45 | 50 |

You can count up to 100 in many other ways. How many groups of 5 does it take to add up to 100? Try **skip-counting** by fives to find out. 5, 10, 15, 20, 25, 30, 35, 40, 45, 50. How many groups of 5 are on this page? Let's keep going!

Now keep skip-counting by 5, starting with 55. So it's 55, 60, 65, 70, 75, 80, 85, 90, 95, 100. Now we know that 20 groups of 5 equal 100!

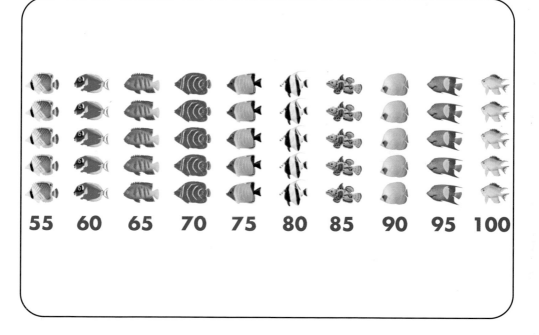

| 55 | 60 | 65 | 70 | 75 | 80 | 85 | 90 | 95 | 100 |

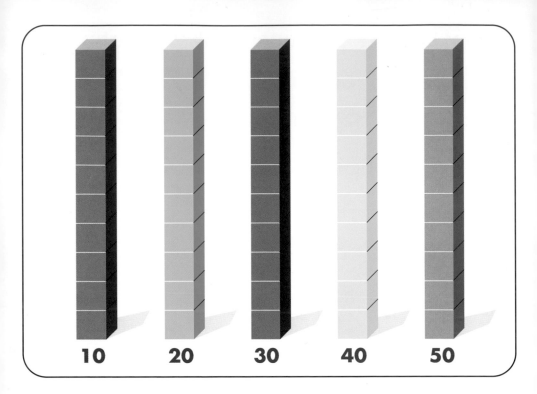

10   **20**   **30**   **40**   **50**

How else can we count up to 100?
Each of these stacks has 10 cubes. Do
the stacks add up to 100? Skip-count
by tens and find out. Start with 10.
Then skip-count to 20, 30, 40, and 50.
You're halfway to 100, but you haven't
reached it yet.

Keep going! Count the first stack on this page starting at 60. So it's 60, 70, 80, 90—100! You added up the stacks. Now you know that 10 tens equal 100!

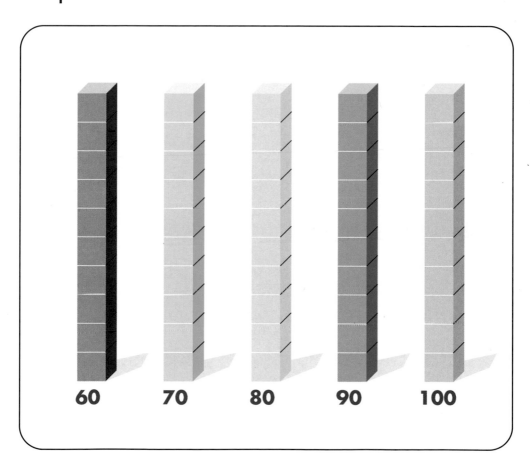

60　　**70**　　**80**　　**90**　　**100**

More or Fewer than 100?

There are 100 seats in this large room. This is the **Senate**. It's where the U.S. senators make the country's laws. When everyone is here, there are 100 people, 1 in each seat.

Baseball games and football games are played in this stadium. Look at all the seats. Compare these seats to the seats in the Senate. Do you think this stadium can seat more or fewer than 100 people?

Do you think there are more or fewer than 100 flowers in this vase? First, take a guess. Then count the flowers by ones, or skip-count by fives or tens to see if you are right.

It would take a long time to count the **total** number of jelly beans in the jar. So, if it's too many to count, then **estimate**. Are there about 100 jelly beans?

Look at all the houses. Now let's take a closer look. How many houses do you think there are in all? Are there more or fewer than 100?

This parade takes place every Thanksgiving. Some people watch the parade on television. Others come out to watch it on the street. How many people do you think are marching in this picture? Are there more or fewer than 100?

100 in Our World

The number 100 is big. Think about what the number 100 means to you. What's the 100th day of school? What month will it be 100 days from now? Is it more or fewer than 100 days until your birthday?

Glossary

digits—any numeral from 0 to 9

equals—means "the same as"

estimate—to guess an amount

number words—the written forms of numbers

skip-counting—counting by groups of twos, fives, tens, etc.

Senate—one of the two houses that make up the U.S. Congress

total—the whole amount

Index

Word Count: 409
Early-Intervention Level: M